*Things I
Didn't Know
Then*

# Things I Didn't Know Then

Abigail Grimes

*Poetry and Prose to shield & save the soul*

WBG/WBC PUBLICATIONS | BOWMANVILLE

Copyright © 2025 by **Abigail Grimes**

All rights reserved. No part of this publication may be reproduced, distributed or transmitted in any form or by any means, without prior written permission.

**Abigail Grimes / WBG/WBC Publications**
**Bowmanville, ON L1C 5C4**
**www.abigailgrimes.com**

Publisher's Note: This is a work of poetry and creative non-fiction. Names, characters, places, and incidents may be a product of the author's imagination. Locales and public names are sometimes used for atmospheric purposes. Any resemblance to actual people, living or dead, or to businesses, companies, events, institutions, or locales is completely coincidental.

Book Layout © 2017 BookDesignTemplates.com

**Things I Didn't Know Then/ Abigail Grimes.** -- 1st ed.
ISBN 978-1-7773863-4-4 Paperback
ISBN 978-1-7773863-5-1 E-Book

This collection is dedicated to those who inspire
the pen and sometimes the sword.
Worlds are built, rise, and fall for you.

This is a work of poetry and prose with themes of love, grief, and loss.
Some stories deal with the subjects of violence, mental health, and thoughts of self-harm.

If you are struggling, please reach out.
In Canada or the US call or text: 9-8-8
24 hours a day / 7 days a week.

Dear Reader,

As you journey through the pages ahead—poems and prose woven with thought, memory, and emotion—I invite you to read not only with your eyes, but with your heart. Let these words meet you where you are.

There is no single way to experience this collection. You may find yourself seen, unsettled, comforted, or inspired. However these pieces speak to you, your response is valid and valuable.

As you turn the final page in this collection, you will find space to write—your reflections, your questions, your sentiments, or simply the silence that remains. It's yours to fill, or not. Let it be a space for whatever flows.

May these pages be both a mirror and a window.

# Contents

The Wounds They Inflict ..................... 1
Little Demon ..................... 3
The Cost of Ice ..................... 5
Nine Letters ..................... 7
Hey Liar ..................... 9
Would You Tell Me? ..................... 11
Extinguished ..................... 12
All Stops ..................... 13
Flicker ..................... 15
3AM Thoughts on Betrayal ..................... 16
The Wounds We Inflict ..................... 19
Delude ..................... 21
Ask Again ..................... 22
Glass House ..................... 24
Distanced ..................... 27
What Does It Take ..................... 28
I Hope I Lied ..................... 29
Figment ..................... 31
Changes ..................... 32
Void ..................... 33
Notes ..................... 35
An Afterword on Notes: ..................... 45

| | |
|---|---|
| Work Life | 51 |
| Confessions in Oz | 53 |
| The Workday Lament | 54 |
| I'm Fine, Thanks. And You? | 55 |
| Team of One | 56 |
| Thief | 57 |
| The Dissonance of Attestation | 58 |
| Love & Romance | 61 |
| Forever You | 63 |
| Pause | 67 |
| Stardust | 68 |
| My Gift | 69 |
| Portrait | 70 |
| Unconditionally | 72 |
| Marshmallows | 74 |
| Behold Her | 76 |
| The Ties That Bind | 79 |
| Come To My Table | 81 |
| Cupboard of Hopes | 82 |
| Safe Harbour | 84 |
| Family Reunion | 85 |
| What Didn't Your Mother Tell You? | 87 |
| All the Things I Should Have Said on a Tuesday Afternoon | 89 |
| Vestiges of my Father | 91 |
| One More Moment | 93 |

Things I Didn't Know Then..................95
Personal Sentiments & Reflections ..................99
Acknowledgements ..........................109
About the Author..................111

# The Wounds They Inflict

*Unwittingly or by Design*

Things I Didn't Know Then

# Little Demon

You bash about
Preying upon those
around you
Like a malevolent spirit

                    You are a poltergeist
               A mooring and chained
                          malcontent
               Doing unto others as you
                 deem has been done to
                                 you

Meting out punishments
measured by
Your once golden, now
tarnished rule
Sullied by acidic clouds
ever-present around you

                    You rest on laurels
            embedded with pins and
                            daggers
             Predicated upon and
             upheld by falsehoods
              woven by charlatans
             They prick at you – mere
               annoyances no doubt

But unsuspectingly slice
deep wounds
Never the same dagger,
but always the same
place
Ensuring you never sit
comfortably

                    Your stability is eroded
            No longer able to discern
              the true nature of harm
                        Imagined or real

In the end,
Little Demon,
You will get what you
deserve

Things I Didn't Know Then

# The Cost of Ice

You will never understand the absolute solitude
   I feel when you lay your eyes on me
How rendered utterly alone it leaves me
My blood freezes
And it's only now, with ice in my veins
I have the strength to leave

As the words pass my lips,
I savour the break in your stony countenance
Finally, proof – albeit but a flash – but proof
   nonetheless
That there, deep in the dank somewhere of your
   soul, still lives a person
Left alone to dim and shrink in the darkness,
Knowing no effort has ever been, nor will ever
   be made to save them

*Someone should help them*

The tiny voice inside calls
My blood warms, and compassion and shame
   wash through me
In that moment, I sense the familiar trap closing
   in
Now, employing the well-observed tactic
I let the ice reset

Abigail Grimes

Left leads the right, and as strides get longer, so
　　does the distance
The distance between me and you
But alarmingly, the distance between me and my
　　inner self
And in the end,
While I am still capable,
I mourn the cost

Things I Didn't Know Then

# Nine Letters

*"Donne-moi un bec la..." A beckoning whisper
floating to my ear whilst sitting curbside at a
depanneur in St. Hubert, Quebec in 1989*


Don't you just want to kiss me?

A question
At times, non-controversial and banal
And others, hopeful – a dangerous accusation

A pause
A playful tease
Equally full of delight and dread

Though in its dangling,
A weapon
In a game no one wants to play

Abigail Grimes

## Sometimes

A simple word
Becomes a deft blade
In a clumsy hand

The beginning of the end
An adverb standing alone
Carrying the weight of a thousand no's

A life envisioned
Splintered into tiny shards of nothingness
And all of it undone, by nine little letters

# Hey Liar

It appears your pantaloons are ablaze again
I wish I knew what purpose it serves for you
For perhaps then I wouldn't be so offended
So taken aback at every turn

I question my investment
The time it takes for the words to spill from your lips
To the time they strike my ear
I must be waiting for insight
Insight, which, sadly, never comes

I am tired
Made to feel Small and Insignificant
Unsteady and Fearful
Surrounded by all the little fires you light around me

Insidious and encroaching
In their multitudes, an inferno
Battle-weary,
I can no longer invest

Abigail Grimes

I'm sitting on a powder keg, and you've got a match
Though you say it's but a feather
I can see the flame
Its malice flickers in the pools of your eyes
And twists your tongue

I am no threat, I assure you
You are safe in my arms
I hold my hands before me, empty of pretense and violence
Full of compassion and forgiveness

A smile,
Your favourite weapon
Then – a whispered fable – 'I love you'
And once more, remorselessly,
We are consumed in flames

Having learned at the foot of the master,
Soul made unassailable over time and Self-shielded deep within
Flames reflect back
And you find you are no longer the only one with a forked tongue

Things I Didn't Know Then

# Would You Tell Me?

You would tell me, right?
Before you leave
You'll tell me?

There will be some warning
Some sounding of alarm
More than the coolness of your touch
The vacancy in your gaze

A message in a bottle
A hieroglyph and decoder ring
A whisper on the breeze
A tap on the shoulder

The one thing I ask
If I am permitted to be so bold
Don't leave
Don't disappear

Not without goodbye
Not before taking a moment to acknowledge
All that lay before you
That which lies behind you

More than fickle moments easily dismissed
A life – albeit one tenuously held together
With bits of string and memories
Tell me, if only to honour those lost things

# Extinguished

The echo of heat is all that remains
    Buried under aloof neglect
    The flame went out

A great fire raged here
    Long ago

Surrounded by trappings
    Sealed on all sides by expectations
    It suffocated

Starkly refusing to acknowledge its existence,
    It starved

Red hot embers glowed
    Then, fuel met water
    Extinguishing what remained of possibility

Without question or pause, sand
    Finality

Snuffed out
    No difference existing between
    Inattentiveness or malicious purpose

There once was a great fire that burned
    And you killed it

Things I Didn't Know Then

# All Stops

Sitting on a train on my standard morning commute
All stops – the express line having been long since revoked
Simply minding my own business
A waft of you hangs in the air on the passing breeze of a stranger.
How did you find me here? After all this time?
I had done so well putting you away
Locking you up tightly in a box of forgotten things
And like the seeping smoke of a demon
Your memory slips from the crevices and snakes its way around my throat,
Stealing into my unsuspecting nostrils.
I absorb you through the very pores of my skin
I feel you twisting—poking round areas you once inhabited
Testing doorknobs, shouting down hallways, until you find that which you seek
Your ethereal tendrils wrap themselves around my heart and squeeze
Unrelenting

Tears threaten, and rapidly blink them away as I buckle under the pressure
I cast a woe-begotten glance after the stranger
Then, turning away, fix my eyes on the middle space between my seat and the window,
Watching the dizzying blur of a world pass by, I pray to be released from your grasp
The opening of the train doors allows for the refreshing exchange of air
The cool gust rinses me clean, a moment of reprieve granted
I am able to, once again, take a breath
12 stops to go
I silently pray no one else has your good taste and my bad fortune

# Flicker

Your hand on mine is like fire
It warms me, reminds me of a life I knew before

Before you
Before this

Now I know for certain the sensation is a lie
The feeling burns within me
It threatens to consume me with rage, with disgust

I barely recognize myself, I have stooped so low
Fallen so far
I can no longer see the light

But I remember

I remember there once was light
Before you there was light

And I will see it again

## 3 AM Thoughts on Betrayal

Betrayal comes in whispers and screams
It lies awake beside you
It follows you throughout your day
It looks you in the eye while it lies
It's in the good mornings and good nights
All the in-betweens
And for a time, you were innocent
Engaged in the farce that played out around you
What happens when the truth comes to light,
    and the betrayal is revealed?
How do you carry on knowing the Betrayers sit
    comfortably alongside you?
Their unspoken lies surrounding you.
Taunting you, relishing in your presumed
    ignorance

~~~

Tired and no longer willing to paint your face
You are no longer willing to play your part
Everything is a question
Was anything genuine?
With no desire to fight you withdraw
No one notices and that speaks volumes
Your plasticine smile was for them
There is no need for it any longer

Things I Didn't Know Then


Curled away, you carve a space for you
Only You.

This is the place where you can scream
Loud enough to shake the Earth
Cry enough tears to quench deserts
And meditate to quiet turbulent seas
It is in this place that you will rebuild,
It is here that you will reclaim the part of your
 heart they tried to steal from you

~~~

When you emerge from this sacred place
You are stronger and wiser
More discerning
Your Betrayers can no longer look you in the
 eye
For they know they will find themselves
 reflected back
And are rendered powerless

~~~

Things won't be the same, and they shouldn't be
But should you need it
The place you created is always there
In the quiet of the middle of the night

# The Wounds We Inflict

*Upon Ourselves and Others*

Things I Didn't Know Then

# Delude

   My problem was
I was still in love with you


                                    And refused to believe
                                  You no longer loved me

# Ask Again

Ask me again
I dare you
Ask me one more time

In jest, or sincerity
In folly, or spite
I dare you

It is plain that it hurts me
It's true I won't call you on it
And you lay comfortable in that knowledge

Paralyzed
By perceived power or privilege
I remain silent in *the knowledge*

Others wouldn't attempt it
To them, I am ferocious
Battle-hardened and dangerous.

But you know what lies beneath
That which no one else can see
No one else would dare

Things I Didn't Know Then

You ask, and though you can't see me
I smile
You dared

Fury rages below the surface
So close to the surface
My teeth shake

I will wait for the moment to pass
For it matters not the number of requests before you
You will push and I will yield

Ask if I'm pregnant
Ask me again
I dare you

So, what's a dare?
Between us?
Hollow. Meaningless.

Until the day it's not
God help you that day
And may He forgive me

# Glass House

There you sit
   Encased in glass
Volatile. Dangerous.
   Watching from your perch

The air fairly sizzles
   Unsettled and frenetic
Passionate
   Conducting from your station

When your eyes fall upon me
   It is revealed
What lay before me is both beguiling and perilous
   To deny it would be a folly

I venture closer
   Excitement pricks my spine
Terrifying. Delicious.
   Untouched from on high

Am I safe?
   Flirting with disaster but knowing it can no longer harm me?
I am safe in the knowledge
   But to whom am I lying?

Things I Didn't Know Then

Encased in glass
   Disarmed
You are far more dangerous than you ever were
   For the boundaries disappear when the threat
   is erased

Take care, I warn
   Protect yourself
The danger lies in the security
   Unblinking and patient, you assess

Glass is fragile
   Fissures lead to cracks
Before the shattered case, I stand
   Shards embedded in my flesh

Unbound and wild
   Unfettered by makeshift limitations
Kinetic charges arch and dance
   You surround me

The true danger of you lies in my imaginings
   You have no hold over me,
But that which I give you
   And to you, I give freely

I surrender
   The battle for not
The long-suffering of a fool realized in vain
   I tend to my wounds

I look again
   There you sit
Encased in glass

Abigail Grimes

Ever disinterested

The truth of the injuries laid bare
    Wounds you watch inflicted upon me,
These gashes upon my psyche and my heart
    Are voluntary

And though we know the truth
    When called before you anon, I shall falter
Battle and succumb
    In our dangerous game

You will sit
    In every iteration, unmoved and self-satisfied
Innocent and treacherous
    Waiting for me to, once more, break the glass

## Distanced

Hold yourself at arm's length
Any closer is sure to spell disaster
So life has taught
Lessons hard earned

Thrice abandoned
Trust, a commodity not easily bestowed
Particularly among those closest
For they betray

Disposable affections, shelved in time
Lack of investment reaps incalculable dividends
A return on investment paid to the deserving
And those decidedly not

Calls for connection unanswered
Fictions fill the void
Until patience breaks through
And comfort can envelope your lonely soul

# What Does It Take

What does it take?
   Everything.

All that you have.
   All of the time.

Here I sit, trying to justify. Rationalize.
   Make peace.

And you – there. No heavy lifting.
   Eager to accept anything I say.

I almost feel bad,
   If it weren't for the hole in me where
     those things used to go.

So, I make the sounds.
   To me – Hollow, Empty.

To your ear, they ring true. You're safe.
   There will come a time when the load is
     laid at your feet.

Will you do the same for me?

Things I Didn't Know Then

# I Hope I Lied

I hope I lied
With my lips, my eyes, my hands
With all the parts of me displayed before you

I hope you couldn't see
How my heart broke
When the lie dictates it be so plumb with joy

I hope my eyes lit up and my lips formed a smile
I hope you couldn't feel the chill run through me
When I wrapped you in my embrace

I fought so hard
To push through the disappointment
The unearned pain

I hope I succeeded
I hope I gave what was expected
What you needed in that moment

Abigail Grimes

The moment the rug was pulled
The moment the ground dropped away


The moment all the possibilities crystallized
    and shattered before me

For the greater good
To lay it all to rest
I hope I lied (and selfishly, I hope you know I
    did)

# Figment

Shadows thrown across the floor
Dance and mingle
Light interspersed, chaotic and violent
Reckless tableaus captured and framed

Figment of imaginings
Deception on display
Vacant, etches of humanity
Far from reach

We are Ghosts
Hollow and untouched
By circumstance and design
Silently shrieking and desperate

Our smiles are falsehoods
They are armour
Yet cruelly, not bulletproof
Though a phantom, there beats a heart

You cannot
You must not
See me
Before I fade away

# Changes

The weight of it
presses and squeezes

The guilt
The awful guilt

My heavy heart
in its boney prison

My disjointed thoughts
bang and crash inside my skull

So many changes
All around

It's inevitable
All of it

So, why does it hurt?
We're only human

Things I Didn't Know Then

# Void


In the void,

                                        I think only of me


And for that,


                      I am utterly ashamed

Abigail Grimes

# Notes

My therapist once told me that I wasn't suicidal. I guess that's good. I hold on to that when times get tough. She came pretty late in the game though. Well after the issues of the past. After the nothingness. But she's a professional so I trust her.

I left my first note when I was quite young. I must have been about nine or ten years old. I had pictured in my mind how it would go before that first note. I had no idea what method I would use. I just knew that I wanted to do it.

Every year my parents used to send us to Montreal to spend a few weeks in the summer with my aunt, uncle, and cousin. My aunt was a schoolteacher and so she had her summers off and could be around to supervise us while my parents worked in Toronto.

My parents would take the train with us to Montreal and return a couple of weeks later to pick us up. My dad worked for the railroad, and we used to travel for free. Something I did not appreciate until the privilege was no longer open to me.

I had written the note prior to one of these trips and while we were gone, my mother found it. I had forgotten all about writing that note, but to this day I will never forget what my mom said to me when she saw me after our summer vacation.

She told me that she found it. I could see the hurt in her eyes, but I could also see the fury. I was too young to understand, but in her eyes, there was also fear. Perhaps it was the fear that I mistook as fury. Perhaps they were the same thing.

The betrayal she felt was something I did not begin to understand until I was well into adulthood. And that understanding came through a lot of patience, time, and questions. She gave up a lot for us and she did a damn good job of covering up that fact. Much to her detriment. And ours. But knowing that now did not help the sting of those words, then.

She called me a coward. She was angry and I am sure she immediately regretted having said something so hateful to a child. Her child. But it stayed with me. A lot of the things she's said over the years have stayed with me, but I don't hate her for it. I truly don't. Today, my mother and I have a great relationship of mutual support, deep love, and appreciation. But at the time when she said those words to me, she might as well have gouged a hole in my soul.

My parents didn't, still don't really, believe in therapy. Why tell a stranger you're hurting? Why tell them your pain? Your weaknesses.

## Things I Didn't Know Then

They will use it against you. Destroy you. Who they were and what their ultimate goal was still eludes me some 30 years later. But we do not talk to strangers. Even if we pay them to listen.

And so, I began to fortify the wall I had previously started to erect around my heart and my mind. If this was not for anyone to see, I would ensure no one would ever reach it. I lay traps on the path to those precious locations. Hidden by mirages and stairs to nowhere. No one would have access. Ever.

My next note was in my mind. I decided when I would do it next, I would write it in blood. No one could say I was a coward then. The writing would, literally, be on the wall. I cried that day, wretched racking sobs as I made my plan. I pictured what the scene would look like. *Am I a coward now?* scrawled in dried blood on the pink bedroom walls I shared with my younger sister. I couldn't bring myself to do it. There were others to consider.

I don't know if I had ever felt so alone.

As the years passed, I bricked the feeling of emptiness and isolation in with the traps around my heart and mind. That little girl still lived inside me, but for a long time she was busy with things to do and sights to see: puberty, high school, and the like. She had things to keep her happy and most important of all, distracted. And when sadness cast its shadow, she was no longer compelled to drop the veil of utter darkness completely.

And that remained the case, until my heart broke for the first time in my life.

This is where things start to sound a bit cliché, but if you are able to put that aside, the dangers of seeing it that way will become quite apparent.

My first couple years of university were exciting and challenging. I had not spent much time thinking about my own mortality during those years, so it came as a bit of a surprise that in a quiet moment of reflection, my roommate asked what scared me the most. Pretty deep for a couple of undergrads, but I was getting in the habit of telling certain people what I really thought – about certain things. So, I answered her. It made me feel incredibly vulnerable, but I looked at her and said that the thing that scared me the most was dying alone.

She laughed that thought off and said that I wouldn't die alone, because I was likely to go in a fiery car crash and she would be my passenger. She knew that wasn't what I meant, but I am not sure I could say that she was wrong. We did go everywhere together, and I did have a bit of a lead foot. We were riding high on youthful exuberance and independence. It was new and wonderful, and we didn't want it to stop. Why sour the mood by talking about death?

It would be years later that I learned of a rumour circulating around my old high school that I had, in fact, passed away in a car accident in another province. Hearing that haunted me for a very long time; and these things would ultimately inspire that sad little girl's newest plan.

The parties, all-nighters, and all the other wild and wonderful things kids get up to when they are away at school were the things that made my life worth every pulse-pounding second. That was, of course, until I fell in love.

I met a boy and he meant everything to me. It was the first time I understood what that actually meant to mean: everything to someone. Over time I took down the wall and dismantled the traps that lay before the fortress that was my heart and mind. Over time I allowed access, complete access, to my soul.

I saw myself in him. And I believe he saw himself in me. We respected each other, cherished each other's successes, and consoled each other when we failed. We supported each other when times were tough, whether the other differed in their view of what tough times were. We respected each other's independence and treasured the time we spent together. It was enriching.

We had a plan for our lives, and it was exciting. He asked my parents for my hand, and we even looked for a house where we would move when we finished school. One that was equal distance from my family and his.

For the first time I could actually envision a future with another person. A true partner. The thought of dying alone had been banished. I was going to grow old with this man by my side, and one day pass away peacefully with our kids and grandkids by my side. A life well lived.

The boy I loved, loved me back for a long time. We were together for four years and they were four of the most important years of my life. There is no denying that. But as things started to fall apart, I fought to keep them together. I tried. I failed.

And when it finally ended, something inside me cracked wide open.

The walls of the fortress that I brought down to love completely had been there for a reason; I had forgotten that reason.

To love fully, everything had to be allowed in. I had been closed to the full spectrum of emotion for too long. I deserved real love, and in order to feel it, I had to be honest. I had to be vulnerable to receive joy and pain, anger, disappointment, and pleasure. I had to allow myself to feel—fully. But in so doing, it left me woefully unprepared for the other side of that feeling. Untethered and unsecured, that sad little girl lashed out and I was lost.

This moment in my life could not have been timed worse if I tried. There was a lot of strife in our family unit; there was no safe haven. I was completely adrift. I needed the pain to stop. I needed a shoulder to cry on, an ear to listen. Arms to squeeze me and someone I loved to tell me it was going to be all right. That I wasn't alone. But I was. My pain was private. No one needed to be inconvenienced by my heartbreak.

## Things I Didn't Know Then

I was falling and did not feel I would ever stop. I was being pulled apart on the inside. I couldn't manage it. I was afraid. I felt I was losing my mind. I felt unloved and cast off.

I had given everything and now I was nothing.

Though the haze in my mind was thick, somehow, I was also practical. I could no longer bear to keep up appearances. I had to go.

I thought of my family and those who would be left behind. How they would handle it. Who would be left to clean up the mess I had created? Who would take care of the arrangements?

I gave it a lot of thought. Would they blame themselves? Would they be angry? With themselves? With me? That gregarious child was no longer in complete control, I was thinking about the consequences of that dark veil. But as time would prove, the time she spent in there unchecked, she had matured.

She had heard a term once and around which she crafted a plan. "Single vehicle collision". It solved everything in one handy package. No one would feel guilty, and the insurance would pay out. No questions. They would be sad, of course, but they would console themselves. She had a lead foot, they would say. Such a shame.

So, in the weeks and months that followed, I set up my insurance policies and made sure there would be no issues.

I knew I couldn't leave a note. It would complicate things.

The day I decided to do it was beautiful. The day previous I had a break down in my parents' room. I let my father see for the first time how much losing this relationship meant to me. He did not know what to do with the outpouring of emotion. I don't blame him; he had never seen it before. He held me for a moment and then stepped back. The hollow inside me ached so badly. I couldn't take it any longer. I knew it was time.

That day I drove to see a friend of mine; she didn't know it was to say goodbye. It was certainly better that way. And on my way home that warm sunny day, with the plan already set, I put it in motion.

Travelling at Autobahn speeds on a 400 series highway is never a good idea, but I needed it to work. And in order for there to be no questions, it had to look like driver error.

There is a place where the highway splits between express and collector lanes and I decided that if it looked like I just made a slight miscalculation it would solve the issue.

I pointed my little silver car at the median and let my mind close.

A transport truck's horn blared. It was the most terrifying sound I had ever heard. And to this day, more than a decade later, the sound unnerves me. It is something I will never forget.

## Things I Didn't Know Then

I will never forget the feeling it gave me. It saved my life that day. An empty, painful life that, at the time, held no value.

My colleagues and I had recently been discussing this taboo, macabre topic in a very academic way. What seemed to resonate most was a particular moment. The moment just before you make the decision that you can't take back. We spoke in general terms about that moment and what it looked like. And most terrifying of all, should you regret the decision in the moment you can't take it back. You can't step back onto the stool, you can't un-pull a trigger. You just can't. The rest is for those you leave behind.

What does the moment before the point of no return look like? For me it looked like a cement barrier in the middle of the highway. It sounded like a truck horn, and it tasted like bile. It felt like ice and blazing fire.

It was the worst moment of my life. It was almost the last moment of my life. And to tell the tale still tightens my chest.

I would be lying if I said that the thought hasn't bubbled to the surface once or twice since, but I know I am in a better place now than I was then. I am able to acknowledge the feelings and work through them; and when I need more support than I can find inside, I seek outside assistance.

I no longer concern myself with what *they* might think. Self-care is desperately important. And I do that by talking. I talk about everything, all the time, much to the chagrin and embarrassment of those nearest and dearest to me. Nowadays, I would much rather see them roll their eyes at me than think about what it would be like to not hear their laughter, share their joy, or support them when they are in pain.

We all make choices we wish we could take back sometimes. We are human, fallible. Our hearts break. We are fragile, but we are also strong. We need one another. Reach out for the help you need. Someone out there, someone you probably know very well, has been where you are, and they will help.

## An Afterword on Notes:

Time has given me the benefit of perspective on this story. Allow me to paint you a picture, and share with you, dear reader, what I learned.

At the time of that crucial moment in her life she was fairly young, but for a young woman she had a very clear view of how her future was to look. A very rigid self-view.

A view that had suffered some hiccups, but one she continued to strive toward with unforgiving, near blind ambition.

Power suits, heels, hair just so. Hanging a shingle – Doe and Co., gaining a fierce and respectable reputation in the community. Walking down marble hallways, saying things like "Your Honour" in a tone that conveyed equal parts respect and admonishment.

A life that saw roles change, where people would come to address her as "Your Honour – and she would be on the receiving end of the tone, only now in a position to give the patient smile from the bench.

She had a vision. It was *her* vision. And then she met him, and for the first time in her life, someone else's vision was important. That is not mean to sound particularly self-centred, she just hadn't been in a position before that moment to contemplate what it would mean to integrate someone else's vision into her own.

Over time, his plan became an integral part of hers.

What she learned about herself was interesting and a little bit sad. It was the first time she ever filled in the picture between school and career with the colour of what a family life might truly look like.

Doe and Co. had a new name – that one was a debate, but they eventually settled on a name they could both live with.

Now, their 2.5 kids would play lacrosse like their mom, and basketball like their dad. They would be smart, sensitive, mature, and terribly cute.

They were an interminable force. A partnership on all fronts.

Life threw some curveballs along the way and the path swerved, but together, they course corrected and kept moving.

There was a new path forward. She became a little forgiving, and learned rigidity in the path meant that she couldn't bend to follow the flow of the river. It meant wonderful things that might have come her way may never find their way to her if she couldn't flow with the course of nature.

Things I Didn't Know Then

When things fell apart, it wasn't just a relationship that fell apart. How she saw herself fell apart.

She turned on herself for becoming soft and unfocused, but most frightening of all, she couldn't see a path forward, nor could she see a path back to the original plan.

It left her untethered from what mattered and from the strides made in her own growth, leaving her angry, melancholic, and unable to forgive herself – she still has issues with self-forgiveness, and while she is in a much better place today, she could never have gotten there if she didn't wake up in that moment.

The rising tides had stolen her breath, and she was choking on the invading waters. The wind bent her to the point of breaking.

She had become rigid.

She tried to course correct but didn't leave room for mistakes. For life. And it nearly cost her everything.

This story serves as a reminder to me, dear reader, that when I think the light is out, I need to give myself a moment to see that it is only dimmed.

To see a way forward, everyday, I have to learn to incorporate all me. All I have learned through the good and the bad.

The resiliency, patience and grace in the face of trials and turmoil are skills innate to me. I just need to lean in and allow my strength to come from the bend, not the rigidity.

    I forgive that young woman for her haste. I respect what it meant to battle with and eventually come to terms with the changing landscape surrounding her.

    I understand her. And mostly importantly, I love her.

Things I Didn't Know Then

# Work Life

*And Other Performative Acts of Drudgery*

Things I Didn't Know Then

# Confessions in Oz

I don't know what I'm doing
   I'm so worried I'll be exposed
They will see the curtain drop

       And laid bare
       Before one and all
       My Secret

Behind the veil
   There's just a parrot and a hamster

       One does the talking
       While the other runs in circles

Abigail Grimes

# The Workday Lament

It's crazy to think how we live our lives

Spending the most creative and fruitful years toiling for "the man"

Spit out at the end, dried husks of shadows of our former selves. Shameful distorted figments our childhood dreams would be ashamed of

Languishing

Creaking bones shuffling to capture glimpses of wonder before our dusty eyes close

Tried and Tired

We press on. Bills, rent, groceries. Wash, rinse, repeat

Underneath it all
But hopeful. Always, hopeful

Things I Didn't Know Then

# I'm Fine, Thanks. And You?

Phalanx position acquired
Nothing gets through
Defences holding
Weary and weathered, we press on

A coordinated assault
Successfully thwarted
Every question an accusation
Every reply, underhanded supposition

Tongue bit clean through
Speech is volatile
Nouns like stones
Verbs, spears

To scratch the surface
Would reveal the pus and grime
The snake (perhaps the ache)
The humanity

Dodging thrusts and parries
Teeth bared, lips split wide
Clown-like in our militant posing
We engage - in polite conversation

Abigail Grimes

# Team of One

My experience is untethered to reality
Demands upon me, endless
Demands upon my time, boundless
Unmoored and set adrift, the ship floats
Directionless
This crew of one is exhausted
Malnourished, unfavoured, and wrung dry
Beset by internal sirens
Imposter Syndrome among their best
Knowing your best is never good enough
Surely doesn't matter
There is nothing to compare oneself to
Set upon by ire
External – a change of pace
Hungry sharks circle close, waiting
The crew will drink of the desiccant sea
Innards wilting
Care all but gone
This team of one expires
Crashed upon the jagged rock
Left to rot amongst other souls
Lost, to corporate malaise

# Thief

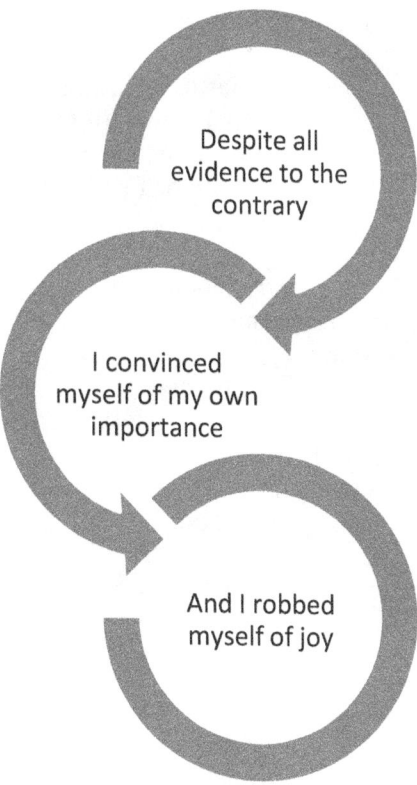

Abigail Grimes

# The Dissonance of Attestation

    Identities
    On a pendulum swing
    To and fro
    Bound in plastic

        Miniature soldiers
        Fight a war with no conviction
        Bodies, once young
        Become bruised and broken

Smiles, once easy
Now fleeting and melancholic
Search for meaning
Amid the din

        Servants and Yes Men
        Jesters and Fools
        Kings and Queens
        All equally beholden

                      Names
                Jostle restlessly
                    To and fro
        Coded legitimacy enclosed
                        therein

Hurried steps denote battle's end
Artifice wanes
Sheathes ripped away
Attestations holstered

## Things I Didn't Know Then

Meaning is found in the periphery
Unvested of the polymer's shackle
Heads rise, and eyes blink, blinded by possibility
Life awaits

Abigail Grimes

# Love & Romance

*And Other Forms of Trickery*

Things I Didn't Know Then

# Forever You

On the breeze
It is only you
In between breaths
It is always you

Fresh tears stain my cheeks
Heal this gaping wound
Sinking in this abyss
Clawing at this vacant expanse

How is it that the world continues to spin?
The sun shines for spite
How dare the birds sing
When the only music was your laugh

Settling at the bottom
The cloaking night heavy upon me
What am I to do?
Now that I have to do it without you

Day broke with a piercing cry
Hearts full and Promise personified
Because of you
A family finally complete

From first steps to peanut butter sandwiches
Bruised knees and goodnight kisses
Shared stories and tender embraces
I wish you angels

I dare not think on it
My tongue twists and lips press shut
Quivering hands reach out
Longing to hold you

Memories repeat
They are both a cruelty and a sanctuary
We were safe and so very loved
We never knew, truly

This sucking wound
Open, yawning
Yet, there is no blood
For all was spilt

My confidant
My closest and truest friend
Untimely ripped from us
From me

The finality of silken-lined oak
The terrible scream of silence
The unfair ebbs and flows of ritual
Wash a tide of solemnity over me

Things I Didn't Know Then

Draped in earth
In response,
A howling chorus of grief rises and surrounds
The world without you

In the close of a kitchen cupboard
Your perfume upon the upholstery
Errand strands of your hair
We feel the absence of you

You kept us afloat
All the unseen things
The unappreciated things
Our strength lay in the quiet of you

I dare not look at the moon
For in its brightness
Your majesty reflects
And I am ashamed

One hollow foot before the other, I step
Cursing the heavens
Begging a forgiveness
Only you can grant

All the ways I need you
All the ways I never loved you
To know now,
The whole of me is gone

Abigail Grimes

I reach deep within to find you
Resting in the unwavering honesty of you
Secured and unmoored by your absolution
I am broken

Silence the crickets
For they needn't commune with you
I thrust myself upon your mercy
My light, my steadfast truth

Hold a place for me
For I cannot yet be where you are
You are an ember in the darkest of night
Warmth where the clutch of cold threatens
never to cease

In every of my remaining breaths
You shall be treasured and revered
For the balance of my life's purpose
Is to honour you

Rest well
In time, I will find you among the stars
And take my rightful place where I belong
Forever with you

Things I Didn't Know Then

# Pause

We find ourselves
In the space between pauses
In moments when the air hangs
Just so
We can see ourselves clearly

We breathe here
Unhurried
Soothed by the faint tell tale pulse
The beat of a heart
Housed just beneath the flesh
Warm and reliable and true

We won't appreciate them – the moments
Not truly
Not until they have passed
The transition so expertly done,
We cede with little resistance

Pulled undertow by shuffling boots on the walk
The discordance of another's tenor
Crammed gracelessly where the pauses once existed
Those moments now a memory,
Lost to the ever-shifting tides of change

# Stardust

We are Stardust,
    Moulded into perfect shapes,
        Unique and beautiful

You have fallen
    So very far from me

Lost
But I will always find you

        The loops and swirls of my fingerprints
A map of the galaxy
    A path back to you

Your signature, etched in the sky
    I will follow
        Until the day you are wrapped in these arms

Home
Safe, among the stars

Things I Didn't Know Then

# My Gift

In the soft bokeh glow
All is laid bare
Guileless, no pretense

The one thing that is plain
Simple and true
Is you

The consistency of you

Stockings hung on the mantel
Before twinkling lights and the crackle of logs on a fire
In the quiet of a snow-covered evening

My one true gift
Found here
In the steady presence of your love

The surety of your hand on mine
The calm inspired by the timbre of your voice
The depth of warmth in your eyes

The unfailing tenderness of you

I am healed and stilled in your closeness
I am seen, comforted.
Blessed

My darling, I adore you

# Portrait

Moments – caught in time
Momentous, mundane
Precious. Abiding.

Now that time has passed
And as only the wisdom of age allows,
Examine what has transpired.

Do it with new eyes
Fresh Eyes
Blessed with humility, purity and tenderness

Time gives the gift of perspective
Patience
Understanding, Sadness and Remorse

~~~

Who can you tell? The secret you see reflected
 there.
Thoughts draped in shame and worry
Expressions of disdain and moroseness

Such a folly.
Who could be convinced that underneath there
 was happiness?
Even joy.

Things I Didn't Know Then


You will try, for posterity, to remember
That which you know now,
That which you could not be convinced of then

*You are beautiful*

~~~

Photographer, I remain haunted by lyrics and
   regret
Never willing to accept you might not take
   another picture

I will smile.
When the time comes, I promise to smile.

Abigail Grimes

# Unconditionally

Months have passed. Years, really.
So many sunsets. Too few words
Greying ringlets spring free from a tightly gathered bun
Betraying the frantic emotion buttoned under a strict façade

Maybe this time I will find the words
Before another fall or winter
Maybe this time, before it's too late
Before he tells me I'm too late

It can't be
It's not fair

The chance to be honest
A chance for once in my sad, detached existence to tell the truth

And it will remain there,
Just shy of my outstretched hand

It's funny sometimes
Time
Life

Brief and Chaotic
Lovely and Splendid
Sordid, yet Rich

Things I Didn't Know Then


We are surrounded by luxuries we cannot begin
to fathom until they are stripped from us
Embrace them,
For time is not among them

I will embrace him
While there is still time
I will embrace him
With truth, with honesty
With Love

But we are not favoured

Moments pregnant with meaning are fleeting
And when the last grains of sand lay spilt from
the hourglass
I will hold him

Precious as it would have been
It will never be
And I will remain, as ever I was

Calm, steadfast, and exacting

In the quiet of space and time, I will let him rest
Uncomplicated, unknowing
Yet all the while, fiercely and silently loved
Unconditionally

# Marshmallows

How you do that
Bring me to my knees with nothing but a glance
The light in your eyes when they fall upon me
I am spotlighted. Seen

Your gaze, it physically touches me
Warms me
I know I am safe, yet I am exposed
How you manage to strip me to my very essence
is remarkable

There is nothing I would hide from you
Before you I am naked
Innocent
Pure

Unfair to those around us / Keep it hidden / The only recourse

You cannot look at me
Not that way

My breath quickens, defenses strip away

You are not mine
I cannot have you - Nor you, me

We mustn't
To give in would mean destruction
Love leaves a terrible wake

Things I Didn't Know Then


If we were to touch, it would engulf us
Then the world
Leaving behind nothing but ashes

For you, I will weigh the consequences

We mustn't
The world will burn

The question measured / The answer Primal

Survival be damned
Bring the marshmallows

Abigail Grimes

## Behold Her

You don't look at me
You used to
Though it was never to see beauty

Was beauty there?
In your eye,
I wonder

Cracks and specks
Errant things
All dissected and discerned, under your eye

All the little things,
The desperate things
The shame-filled things

Left to wonder
How desperate I was
To have your eyes upon me
Undiscerning - a simple, admiring gaze

Hopeful for the day
That one fateful day when they would behold
Something desirous
Something beautiful

Then the day came
When I saw past you
And saw, maybe for the first time,
Myself

## Things I Didn't Know Then

Avert your eyes

Every scrape and scar is a story

The tale of me.
A fable.
A Myth.

A romance in the stretches and pulls of my
   skin
A parable in the arc and camber of my walk
Speaking with Confidence

A legend
That tells of Resilience, and Sacrifice
And Love

In the shadow that follows,
The echo of Wisdom
And Patience

My shoulders, pillars,
For those who come after to rise upon
And know heights of which I could only
   conceive

A life, chronicled before you,
but not for you

I reach back to the girl
Once so unsure in her steps,
And welcome her to my bosom
I remind her of the footfalls
That brought us to this place

Abigail Grimes

A life no other steps could have led her
A journey that had it been walked by another,
Would never lead them to where she stood
   today

It is with Pride and Humility
Gratitude, and Strength
That I stand before you

Those footsteps formed a path just my own
For the path is as unique as the prints
Gracing the tips of my fingers
And though at times challenging,
Each step ensured growth and understanding

Cast your gaze this way, I invite you
But be not confused,
Its judgments hold no weight here

Behold the wonderment in creases
And streaks of silver

All the things you claim failed you
Were never for you from the start

Each revelation, a tiding,
An account,
The very evidence of my success

There,
In the sum of it all,
There lies Beauty

Behold her.

# The Ties That Bind

*Where Our Hearts Come to Rest*

# Come To My Table

Come
Let us sit
Together,
At my table

Drink with me
Without fear
Supp with me
With no reprisals

Share with me
Commune
With me

So I know,
I am not alone

Together,
Let us be comforted
Together,
We are not alone

## Cupboard of Hopes

A bag of sweet, dark Demerara sugar
Rolled closed and held securely
With a rubber band from Chinese food leftovers
Stashed in the cupboard

You put them down
Just for a moment
One day after the shopping
With the curry powder and salt

One day, like any other day
When you were a person
With hopes and schemes
Before the *every* day of the everyday began

You put them down
Just for a second

Hidden in the back,
Nestled behind black pepper and smoked paprika
They sit patiently

Off to the cupboard
For a dash of this
A sprinkle of that

Things I Didn't Know Then


Plates prepared fit for royalty
Artfully conjured with skill and devotion
Bewitching hungry mouths who share your eyes and nose and curiosity
Proudly, this becomes the every day of your everyday

All the while,
The dreams you made
Shift further back in the cupboard
Resting there, waiting upon
Whispered promises made to one day return

Ingredients come and go
Cupboards refresh
And you fix and fiddle
Remembering and repositioning silent vows

Years pass
The nest empties
Shelves, no longer overloaded
Display what had, for so long, been set aside

Now face to face who you meant to be
I bid you, know it's not too late
Dust off the label
Keep your word

And, as you've done
With all ingredients that touched your hand over the passage of time,
With compassion and grace,
Make magic

Abigail Grimes

## Safe Harbour

Rest
For you are safe here
Though storms may rage against you

Trust
For you are safe with me
I am your anchor

When carried away on life's rapids
Its fateful twists and devilish turns
Look to me

The rooted branch,
Outstretched and still
Firm, in the midst of chaos

Reach for me
Hold steadfast unto me
For here, you are protected

Til rushing waters turn to calm
In times of great trouble or doubt
From wonderous joy to the depths of sorrow

I remain
Forever
Your safe harbour

Things I Didn't Know Then

# Family Reunion

    Hands, scarred and wrinkled
        Nails cracking in odd places

    Stress laid bare
        All the pressure points revealed

    Hair that greyed too early
        Out of place and yet, uniquely, just so

    Unlike her mother and everything of her father
        Except upon further inspection

    His wit / Her face
        Her generosity / His temper

        No patience - but that's no surprise

    Clumsy and studious
        Impulsive and diligent

    Tall, like him
        Wide, like her

        Smart and naive - measured in equal parts

Abigail Grimes

Granny's determined eyes
    Grandma's adventurous heart

Grandfather's mischievousness
    Granddad's call to sea air

Two left feet and anything but graceful
    A heart of gold with a venomous smile

I carry in me the past, present, and future
    A beautiful walking contradiction

    A family portrait etched on a canvas of flesh
        and bone

Things I Didn't Know Then

# What Didn't Your Mother Tell You?

What didn't your mother tell you?

Standing squarely in my middle age I wonder
    About all the things your mother never told you
        Things you were forced to discover on your own

Did you ever tell her?

In the letters you never sent
    Were the words there?

In those sentences filled with awe and wonder
Those sentences chockful of anxiety and grief
    Did you tell her?

When you came here
    Not more than a girl
Were you as full of piss and vinegar as I was
    when I met that age?

Did you hold your head high and square your shoulders to every challenge?

> Were you terrified?
> Like I was?

In the letters that never made it to her hands
Did you ask her what she thought she was protecting you from?

Did you reason, as I have, that she was just as naïve as you?
> That she was just a girl, doing the best she could
> And that to paint your reality with her fears would do you no good?

Did you forgive her?
For all the things she didn't tell you?

For silently wishing you happiness and blessings
> For trusting your will and determination
> For waiting on word, all the while beaming with pride

Though words went unspoken, though oceans apart
> I hope you step forward assuredly, knowing, as I do, you were loved with her whole heart.

Things I Didn't Know Then

# All the Things I Should Have Said on a Tuesday Afternoon

Smiles lay heavy upon our lips
Our mouths empty caverns through which jumbled alphabets clamour and spill
Forming sharp stalactites and mighty stalagmites
Forging treacherous paths
Over time, from below and above fuse to impressive columns of silence, containing all the things never said

As we grow, we tread old patterns on new paths
Search through rubble to find jewels to polish and shine
To string together meaning to lay like wreaths upon our weary shoulders
Strings to pass down, so they won't be lost

Adorning ourselves in words, in hopes that someone will see.
Someone will call attention.
Someone will deem them valuable.
All the while knowing they are but glass
Shiny and pretty; Fragile and meaningless

Abigail Grimes

Sitting together in silence we claim is comfortable
We share a drink in the summer sun
Watching perspiration form upon the glass

Droplets catch in the sun and sparkle, the way
    conversation should

The heavy smile returns, carrying the weight of
    deep yearning
Desperate to chip away at the façade
Eyes now cloudy with time and knowing
Starkly aware that it's too late

Silent vows to do better brush against reality
There will be no opportunity
There will be no other time
Never to admit we are so terribly alone

Glass beads draped against my collar,
Once yawning caves, now sewn shut
I sit
With all the things I should have said on a
    Tuesday afternoon

Things I Didn't Know Then

# Vestiges of my Father

My first gift,
As I drew my first breath,
Your name

Your hand,
At once strong and gentle
Guides a path through life's dense forest

Marking a trail
Leaving an indelible mark on my heart and mind

Moulding my thoughts,
Allowing space for growth
Encouraging loving critique

You watch with patient eyes
At the multitude of mistakes and corrections
Made along a road you once trod

Offering grim tales and doses of wisdom
Couching stings with a humour I now proudly
call my own

Abigail Grimes

Never further than a thought,
I rely on your insight,
Trust your counsel,
And admire your silence

Ever chasing shadows,
Seeing life a generation out of step
When I grow up, I can't wait to meet you

Things I Didn't Know Then

# One More Moment

Tested to the limit
Endured all they could

In the end measured and found themselves wanting

Life weighed against perceptions of perceptions

Tried and tired
Heartbroken
They left us behind

What we wouldn't give for but one more moment

To forgive, to forget
To linger in a gaze, to share a smile
To hear and to be heard

Just one more

Abigail Grimes

To sit together in silence
To listen with our entire beings with open, compassionate hearts

To hold
To love

Life is not convenient
Its lessons come fast and are often harsh

Do it now
Say it now

Love now
Time does not wait

## Things I Didn't Know Then

Dear Briar,
There are so many things I didn't know at the time.

The day I truly said goodbye to the idea of feeling your first kick was the same day I would be grateful someone answered the call and rolled up their sleeve to save a life.

When I was first asked why I donate, I hadn't been on the receiving end of the gift. I knew people who had, and while that was a compelling enough reason, I simply felt a personal responsibility to help, to find a way to give back.

Those who asked didn't know it was going to be me who would come to need it.

I didn't know either.

But as things go, even the best-laid plans can go awry, causing a great deal to be on the line.

A lot of people were instrumental that day to ensure my eyes opened.

Unsung professionals who, until I read the report later, I never knew were in the room when I was slipping away – following you.

I am grateful to them, and I am grateful to you for allowing me to reflect upon all the elements of that fateful day.

Without them, I wouldn't be here to tell you how much I miss you. I wouldn't be here to try to make the most of the second chance giving you up would afford me.

I just hope I am living my life in a way that makes the sacrifice worth it. In a way that would make you proud.

Reflecting back and paying it forward is my way.

You – in the form of the greatest sacrifice I ever made – are, in a most significant way, a large part of my ability to do so.

Briar, my dearest, always with a humble heart, thank you.

Love,

Me

Things I Didn't Know Then

Abigail Grimes

## Personal Sentiments & Reflections

Poetry has a way of touching the quiet corners of our lives—stirring memory, emotion, and thought. Pause and let the words echo beyond the page.

In the space that follows, I invite you to let the conversation between you and the collection continue.

Write with an open heart.

Thank you for spending time with this collection.

Yours, with gratitude,

Abigail

Things I Didn't Know Then

Personal Sentiments & Reflections

Things I Didn't Know Then

# Personal Sentiments & Reflections

Things I Didn't Know Then

Personal Sentiments & Reflections

Things I Didn't Know Then

Personal Sentiments & Reflections

Things I Didn't Know Then

Personal Sentiments & Reflections

Things I Didn't Know Then

Personal Sentiments & Reflections

Things I Didn't Know Then

Personal Sentiments & Reflections

Things I Didn't Know Then

Personal Sentiments & Reflections

Personal Sentiments & Reflections

# Acknowledgements

Thank you to my family and friends for their encouragement, support, and patience during the many days and nights I spent working on and talking about this collection.

Thank you to Anil Kamal for your sensitive eye and skilled hands. I know my work is always made better by your keen suggestions and the deft stroke of your pen.

# About the Author

Abigail Grimes is a Canadian multi-genre author of fiction and poetry.

Living in rural Ontario and working in the bustling metropolitan city of Toronto, Ontario, she finds inspiration in the diverse settings around her.

A featured author at the Salon of the Refused, BlackLit Durham, and the Northumberland Festival of the Arts, Abigail is the author of the thriller *The Violence of Fire* and the poetry and prose collection *For The Quiet*, available wherever you buy books.

For stories, musings and more, check out [abigailgrimes.com](abigailgrimes.com).

www.ingramcontent.com/pod-product-compliance
Lightning Source LLC
Chambersburg PA
CBHW020009050426
42450CB00005B/384